THE
HUMAN
AVIARY

Photographs by
GEORGE HOLTON

Text by
KENNETH E. READ

A Scribner Portfolio in Natural History

THE HUMAN AVIARY

A Pictorial Discovery of New Guinea

CHARLES SCRIBNER'S SONS · NEW YORK

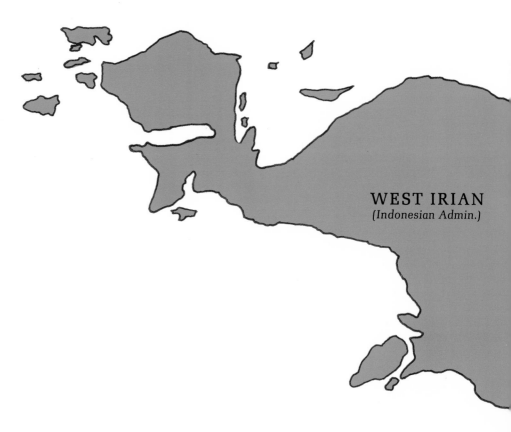

WEST IRIAN
(Indonesian Admin.)

New Guinea, showing some places mentioned or illustrated in the book

THE
HUMAN
AVIARY

TERRITORY OF PAPUA AND NEW GUINEA

(Australian Admin.)

SEPIK Maprik •

Sepik R.

Angoram •

NEW GUINEA

WESTERN
HIGHLANDS

Wabag •

Mt.
Wilhelm

Wahgi R.

Asaro R.

CHIMBU

Mt. Minj •
Hagen •

EASTERN HIGHLANDS

Markham R.

PAPUA

FLY R.

Purari R.

Gulf of Papua

NEW IRELAND

NEW BRITAIN

TROBRIAND IS.

D'ENTRECASTEAUX IS.

• Port Moresby

Early morning in a village near Mount Hagen, Western Highlands

 Islands have always fascinated men. Why they exercise this compelling attraction remains a mystery, but perhaps it has something to do with a yearning to return to more innocent and less complicated beginnings, to a time when the circumference of the world was no larger than the boundaries of a tribal territory and the men who lived within it depended personally on one another. Now, as man leaves this planet, he looks back on the island earth, seeing it as no other generation has ever viewed it—a fragile, peacock-jewel floating in the dark immensity of space.

New Guinea, however, is not an island to which the imagination has responded with this tender recognition. Its very size modifies the feeling of vulnerable isolation that islands convey, and its shape suggests a nightmare fantasy rather than the gentle visions of a daydream.

Second in area only to Greenland among the islands of the world, it rides the warm seas north of Australia like a prehistoric mother bird marshaling a fledgling flock that spreads behind it to the boundary of Polynesia. Its great head points toward its Asian homeland, and in the early morning, as it stirs beneath the covers of its clouds, the air seems to be filled with its ruminations on the themes of men and time. It existed long before man found protection under its rainbow plumage. The millennia in which he counts his journey from his primate origins are less than a single heartbeat of its own life, and like an ancient, symbolic elder it stands aside, reserving its judgment on the divided nature of this recent species.

It was sculpted in Paleozoic times, and its face still bears the imprint of the giant fingers that fashioned it out of malleable clay. It is not a gentle land, and it has not come gently into the second half of the twentieth century. Above all, it is a land of contrasts, from the moist and insect-laden estuaries of overburdened rivers to the white sigh of coral beaches; from the undersea cathedral silence of trackless forests to the heady atmosphere of high-altitude valleys where sun and clouds project kaleidoscopic visions of the first day of creation. Its colors startle. Curiously marbled leaves could be laboratory cultures of delicate tissues magnified a thousandfold by the lens of light.

The crimson veins of a caladium leaf, magnified by dew

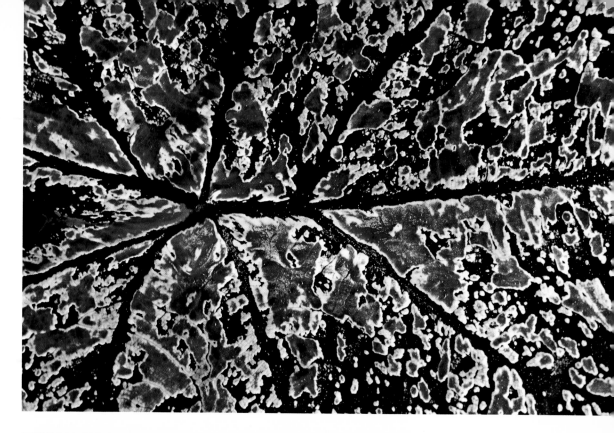

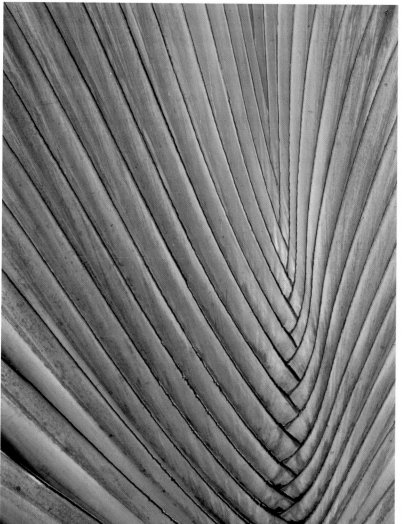

Exuberant coastal foliage
throwing patterned screens
across the light

Leaf of the traveler's palm,
so named because its sap
provides a refreshing drink

9

Green moss hangs from the trees like mermaid hair, and far below, phosphorescent colonies on the humus-laden floor of the rain forest bring to mind the waters of the reefs where gardens of marine creatures move in timeless counterpoint to the lift and fall of the ocean.

The men New Guinea shelters are as varied as its natural features. No comparable area of the earth's surface offers so great a variety of languages and customs. It is a huge "aviary" for a species whose contrived plumage rivals the birds that flash like vivid thoughts through the vaults of the jungle. As the people gather for a celebration, the emerald grass and the bare earth of village streets blossom with creatures conjured from Prospero's island in *The Tempest*. The sky fills with tossing feathers. The universe resounds to cries that are torn from the caverns of the psyche.

Birds and men: the two are not equated merely for literary effect. In the valleys that lie within the western mountains, the Dani-speaking people liken themselves to birds, contrasting the brief and darting brilliance of both with the snake that sheds its skin to be reborn from year to year. More transient than snakes, men and birds die once and for all, and death is a familiar to the people of New Guinea. Since men first found their way to that island,

Green tree python

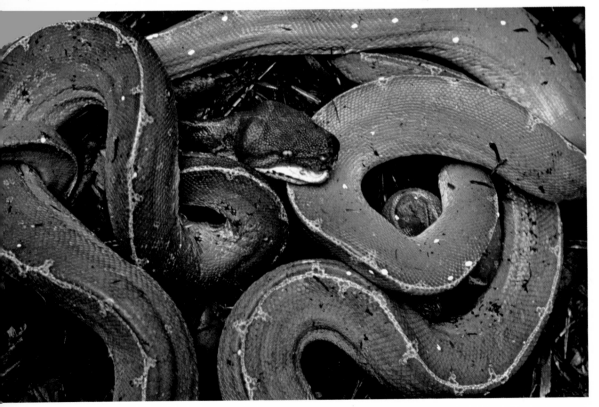

there have been no larger animals for them to hunt. They have fought one another, as men, apparently, have always fought—blind to the kinship of their species. Yet their warfare lacks the gross, impersonal slaughter that advanced nations have inflicted on each other. The bow and spear have perpetrated nothing equivalent to the enormities of the Second World War—the fire-bombing of Dresden and the faceless, terrifying holocaust of Hiroshima. Death in New Guinea, however it may come, remains a personal issue, not a weekly score recorded against a background of national flags. Rather, it is an event that cries for protest, protest for the ties of a lifetime that have been so arbitrarily sundered. The golden corpse, seated in its enclosure of leaves, offers a white grin to the world, a rending coda to the end that waits for all of us.

Men and birds: it is more usual to speak of the kinship between man and other terrestrial creatures, but New Guinea is a land where surprises are an everyday occurrence. And, after all, what are the Dani saying that is different from the knowledge that men have tried to express, often in far more words, through the countless centuries since they were gifted with the dubious powers of self-awareness? Earth and air, flesh and spirit—these are the poles that have governed our erratic course since life emerged on our planet. No subsequent generation of man has effected a viable reconciliation between them, but air is the element to which all have aspired.

Bird of paradise in display

Eclectus parrot (female) on a pepper vine

Men of the Wahgi Valley, Western Highlands, decorated with bird of paradise
feathers for a dance

A man from Minj in the
Western Highlands

A man from Lake Kopiago,
Western Highlands. The badge
on his forehead, a replica of
the Australian coat of arms,
indicates that he is a
government-appointed
headman

14

Victoria crested (or guria) pigeons

Sulphur crested cockatoo

The men of New Guinea have always lived close to the earth. In many ways, the tenor of traditional life is an echo of Western civilization's rural past. Time is not cut into the small measures of hours and minutes. Its markers are not the impersonal hands of a clock, but day and night, the position of the sun and the constellations, the cyclical life of marine creatures, the seasonal variations in the edible products of soil and trees. Time flows as nature dictates, and men respond to it, rather than imposing their will upon it.

They build their houses close to the resources that sustain them. In many coastal areas, their colonies extend into the sea, raised on piles above the glitter of the variegated water—Venices of pole and thatch where a child's first visions of the world include the rippling of the light reflected on the underside of roof and rafters. Inland, their villages and homesteads lie in

Coastal village on the Gulf of Papua, at low tide. Ladders give access from the sea to the verandas of the houses

the midst of cultivations where root crops—yams and taro and sweet potatoes—are husbanded with care and affection. For food—domesticated pigs and garden produce—is more than essential nourishment. It is wealth as well, a source of great pride, of individual and group prestige.

So the Trobriand islanders east of the main island of New Guinea build "treasuries" in their villages in which to store their yams, buildings as carefully constructed and decorated as the great Amish barns of Pennsylvania, which similarly reflect the life values of a people. It is appropriate that these island storage houses watch over the flux of daily life, for throughout this varied country the presentation and distribution of food is a necessary accompaniment to every significant event, recurring month to month and year to year like an insistent, basic drumbeat, punctuating the narrative of every life. Birth is so celebrated; then first menstruation and

A small boy in the Trobriand Islands taking shelter under an "umbrella" made of dried leaves of the pandanus palm. The canoe is filled with yam tubers

male initiation, which divide the sheltered world of childhood from the assumption of adult responsibilities; marriage, the enduring human institution whose roots lie in social rather than biological needs; and finally death, when all those to whom one has been bound pay their last respects to a life that has been interwoven with their own.

Relatives gathered around the gold-colored smoked corpse of a man of Wapanemanda, Western Highlands

A woman in mourning,
Mount Hagen

In the Western Highlands, relatives gathered for the funeral of a kinsman.
To show their grief they have coated their bodies with ocher

Food—the wealth it signifies, the skill and industry it demonstrates—is the focus of all the great festivals that interrupt the tenor of ordinary life like a sudden acceleration of the heart. In the Eastern Highlands, months, even years, of careful preparation and husbandry, of judiciously weighing debts and resources, precede the vast slaughter of pigs to be presented to the invited guests as a proclamation of achievement having both secular and sacred connotations. In the low-lying valley of the Markham River, the harvested yams are borne to the villages on decorated litters shouldered by excited men and placed on towering conical frames surmounted by banners of colored cloth that draw the eye upward, even as the plumes of medieval knights were intended to inspire their rivals with respect and awe.

Sometimes the display of food and the avid interest it evokes seem as vulgarly ostentatious as the Roman banquets depicted in the first century of our era by Gaius Petronius in his *Satyricon*. Indeed, cultural anthropologists report that among some groups the hallmark of a host's success is to feed his guests until they vomit. Even the smell of rotting food is said to produce euphoric emotions. Allowing for some overstatement on the part of the informants, there is no mistaking the intense preoccupation of men and women surveying the carcasses of pigs, the harvested yams, the displays

A mortuary exchange in front of yam storehouses; Trobriand Islands

Storehouses for harvested yams,
Trobriand Islands

Detail of decoration on the outside walls,
of a yam storehouse, Trobriand Islands

21

of other produce. The associations aroused go too far back, even without the differences in cultural idiom, for Westerners to "know"; for these vegetables and slaughtered animals are symbols of common goals and aspirations, standing for whole systems of social relationships. They are even statements

of a cosmic viewpoint, testifying to man's dependence upon powers that transcend his limited capacities. They are linked to culture heroes and to myths of creation, joining the vulnerable world of man's devising to the "otherworld" of timelessness.

Yams and bananas displayed for an exchange of wealth at a marriage

Daily life is no more spectacular than it is in any other part of the world. It consists mainly of routine activities, repetitious and rather dull, revolving around the management of resources. The people toiling at their fishing nets, constructing garden fences, weeding between the rows of vines, are drab shadows of the brilliantly painted figures that at times of festival tread the dancing grounds and village streets like animated and hieratic images.

The day begins early. In the high, interior valleys people are astir when the world is like a primordial seascape, when the contours of the ranges lift above their settlements like blue waves momentarily frozen in their forward motion. They move like wraiths through the spume of rising mists,

"Butterfly" fishing nets drying in the sun at the edge of a lagoon, Trobriand Islands

24

Early morning in the village of Angoram, Sepik River

hugging their naked chests against the chilly air, often grumbling as people do when they try to rise above the surface of sleep, and in their self-preoccupation giving sharp replies to the thin-voiced demands of children. When their bones are warm again, when they have eaten some cold leftovers from the previous evening's meal, they shake off the dreams of the night and turn to the business of living.

This is mostly toil, but not the impersonal toil of mass assembly lines in vibrating factories. The men who cast the lacy nets into the turquoise waters of a lagoon, the crew of a canoe traveling the morning surface of a river, the women whose hands are wet with the dew that bends the leaves of vines, the chattering groups cutting and tying the russet grasses to thatch the roof of a new home—all these are working together because of personal ties. No one is anonymous. The division of labor and the decisions as to who assembles for a given task are determined by a wider system of relationships that binds the individuals to one another. The joint activity is one of the ways in which these bonds are expressed. Work is not only necessary to survival, it is also a daily demonstration of dependence on one another, a strand in the web that begins with birth and, among some peoples, continues beyond the grave.

Other than the assignment of certain tasks according to sex, there is virtually no economic specialization anywhere in New Guinea. Some persons, naturally, are more skilled than others at various tasks—more skilled in perceiving the shape and the dimensions of a canoe in the living column

25

of a tree, more skilled in carving the intricate barbs of an arrowhead, in sensing the balance of the shaft for a spear, in aligning the rafters of a roof. But these aptitudes have not become embalmed in full-time professionalism. There are no artisans, merchants, or middlemen who repair regularly to their shops or their stalls in an established marketplace. No one is exempted from

the grubby chores of producing the food that sustains them all. Traditionally, there was no wage labor. Those who assisted in the building of a house brought their own contribution to the meal that celebrated its completion, as neighbors did at barn raisings in early unindustrialized America. Labor is an obligation that helps to flesh the skeletal framework of a community.

A dug-out canoe, the means of transportation on the Sepik River

(Right) The bow of a dug-out canoe, carved in the shape of a crocodile's head

Another carved canoe bow, with the figure of a man lying on the crocodile's head

This framework is extraordinarily diverse, but in every group the family—husband and wife and their children—is the basic unit. Qualitatively and structurally, it is not necessarily a replica of the group that we identify as the family. Indeed, in the Trobriand Islands, according to anthropologist Bronislaw Malinowski, the first to study these people in depth, it was not perceived as a "biologically connected group"; in Trobriand belief, sexual intercourse had nothing to do with conception. While this extreme view is not characteristic for New Guinea as a whole, it is reflected to some degree in an assertion that conception cannot result from a single sexual act; the child has to be "made" by repeated intercourse. In the Asaro Valley of the Eastern Highlands, a youth charged with responsibility for the pregnancy of an unmarried girl will often rest his defense on the ground that he could not be the father of her child because he had slept with her only once.

Domestic arrangements are mostly, though not always, the kind with which we in the West are familiar—parents and children sharing a common dwelling. In many highland groups, however, a husband did not sleep in the house his wife occupied but retired to a special clubhouse and the company of other initiated men, a custom reflecting widespread beliefs concerning female pollution and an opposition, often dangerous, between the sexes. Indeed, although the values that we load upon the family—often with great strain to the relationships of its members—are all recognizable in New Guinea, they are not so narrowly focused. Husband and wife form both an economic and a sexual partnership. The care and protection of children is one of their joint responsibilities. Physical attraction is also important, even though most first marriages are arranged, and as couples mature and their lives grow together, deep companionship is a frequent dividend.

A Trobriand Islands family

Chimbu mother and child, Western Highlands

The family, however, is not the isolated and vulnerable cell that it has become in mass society. It is only one cell in a body of kinsmen that may include scores of other people, even everyone who lives in one's home settlement and most of those whom one is likely to encounter through the passage of a routine day. Notions of kinship cast a wide net into the sea of human beings, drawing both people and localities together in groups that are part of the way in which each person learns to view the world. This world is small, often no more than the circumference of a circle described with a radius of ten miles from the center where one was born. But within these limits it is mapped by personal ties. Its continents and countries may be clans or other kinship groups. Its conventional coloration is not the gross dimensions of national states but the neighborhoods of people to whom one is bound by birth and marriage.

In this circumscribed world, a man may move with relative security. He knows the type of welcome he will receive in a given place and, if he is wise, he avoids those places where he is a stranger. For his world, no less than our own, is a divided one. Even within its narrow spatial limits there are enemies, people or groups of people who are opposed to him, who for motives of self-aggrandizement and "patriotic" chauvinism regard his life as a legitimate forfeit. Man in New Guinea lives, as all men do, in a state of ultimate uncertainty concerning the actions of his own kind. In a way, his situation might be construed as one of the most telling indictments of his species, for, apart from an occasionally enraged boar or a slumbering viper, there are no other animals large enough or sufficiently aggressive to fear. In his local wars, which sometimes resemble the ceremonial of medieval jousting, one may be tempted to see an innate, species-wide predisposition: man the destroyer of his own kind, the herd animal protecting his territory, born with blood on his mind, carrying within him the chemistry of a killer ape, a species whose opposable thumb allowed its members not only to construct fine tools but also to fashion and handle weapons of their own contriving.

There is a certain irony in the fact that most of the local cultures are very "American." With extremely few exceptions, there are no hereditary positions of authority, no "chiefs" whose power derives from the accidents of birth or class. The pyramidal class structures of Polynesia, with their courtly procedures reminiscent of Versailles in the reign of Louis XIV, never existed in New Guinea. Men rose to influence on their merits, prompted by the imponderables of ambition and their own demonstrated skills. Perhaps

Grandfather and grandson, Maprik, Sepik River

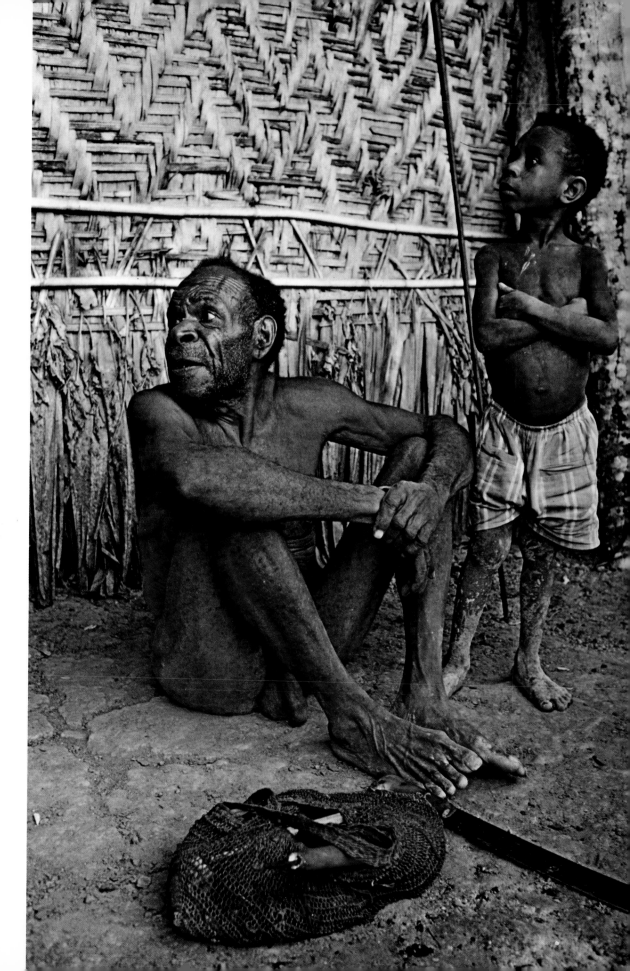

A simulated game of warfare in the Chimbu area

foremost among these skills was the ability to accumulate wealth. New Guineans were, and are, materialists.

In the vast majority of their cultures worldly success has been a necessary yardstick for public influence and reputation. There were no yawning differences in wealth such as those that divided a Medici, a Jay Gould, or a Rockefeller from other segments of the population. Traditionally, wealth did not represent a finer house or greater material comforts, but rather, as with a ward heeler dispensing political patronage, the ability to attract a following of people who would listen when one spoke. These followers were bound to such a leader in a mesh of obligations stemming from his contributions to their marriages, their births and deaths, and the grand occasions of community life. Throughout this difficult country, the leader was the "big man," the person who had "made it" according to the values of his group.

One should remember this as one watches with astonishment the moving frieze of figures garbed like Assyrian kings, weighted by necklaces of sun-reflecting shell, their limbs concealed under the heroic folds of ceremonial dress, their faces static masks for lively eyes, their heads bedecked with fur and brave feathers. For these are not figures in a carnival, in a Mardi Gras promoted by experts in public relations. They are statements of a whole way of life, grandiose and prideful, vaulting and assertive, living monuments

Men of the Enga people, Western Highlands, in ceremonial dress. Their wigs are made of human hair, their long "skirts" of netted vegetable fibers. Since they live far from the coast (many have never seen the ocean), their shell ornaments—important valuables—reach them over extended trading routes

to human themes that other cultures have attempted to enshrine in imperishable stone and marble. A bearded man looks into the camera through a visor of paint that transforms his face into a startling duplication of the hollow-cheeked, triangular heads of European Gothic sculpture—the Christ in ivory or the effigy of a king on the lid of a sarcophagus under the twilight arches of a great cathedral. Caught in a moment of watchful rest against a cloudless sky are three figures, obviously young, the dark silk of their skin punctuated with the whiteness of bone ornaments and the airy splendor of plumes from a creature whose very name, the bird of paradise, is an echo of some universal feeling of a lost and irretrievable innocence. They could be young esquires attending Henry VIII or Francois I at the Field of the Cloth

(Left) Man from Lake Kopiago in ceremonial dress. Body painting, reflecting personal tastes, is characteristic of all the people of New Guinea

Kukukuku men from the Eastern Highlands in ceremonial dress of shells and bird of paradise plumes

of Gold. At the sight of them the heart seems to quicken, as to trumpet sound and the flourish of heraldic tabards, the gold-laced promenade of knights and the formal quadrilles of a diplomacy in which the guiding principle is never to lose, never to admit that another is your equal.

These iridescent congregations of people, flocks of bizarre creatures reminiscent of illustrations in a medieval bestiary, who seem to settle on the dancing ground like birds alighting on the bare branches of a tree, these scintillating, shouting, drum-beating, earth-pounding human beings are expressing a commitment probably as old as man, a parochial commitment to the grandeur and the accomplishments of the group, which out from tribal beginnings, as the world shrank, resulted in militant nationalism.

(Right, above) A Minj ''warrior'' with a decorated shield. The colors are not the traditional earth and vegetable dyes but commercial pigments brought in trade stores

(Right, below) Man from Wabag, Western Highlands. His wig, a characteristic male adornment in his culture, is made of human hair placed on an intricate frame and decorated with parrot feathers and everlasting blooms

Enga men massed at a dancing ground

This is possibly the basic message one should read in the ebony face veiled in a chain mail of golden spots or the glowing quarterings that might have adorned the tunic of an emissary striding the rush-lit hall of a border castle. Here are the pride and the conviction of greatness that have raised obelisks and pyramids, built an Arc de Triomphe and enshrined a brooding Lincoln in a neo-Grecian temple—and also sent armies marching against each other across the face of the globe, fired neighborhoods in the squalor of riots, and led to the terrifying, programmed extermination of Dachau.

This is the cautionary and seemingly endless lesson behind the prancing figures whose brilliant dance frames are not only an extension of the self but also, in their massed array, a demonstration of strength that is cousin to the rumbling armaments and the cohorts of banner-holding youth passing the reviewing stand at Lenin's tomb on May Day—a date shrouded in ancient myths and perpetual human hopes for renewal.

Ceremonial face decoration, Chimbu area

Bena-Bena man from the Eastern Highlands with dance-frame and headdress of opossum fur, shell, and feathers

Men from the Asaro Valley, Eastern Highlands, with dance-frames of bark-cloth stretched over a cane form, painted and decorated with feathers

 Such myths and hopes are also reflected by the gorgeously attired dancers. For characteristically man's great festivals were not merely secular ceremonies; rather, they were also celebrations of a timeless suprahuman order, traditional expressions of a basic posture of man—a species possessing unique capacities but also aware of his limitations, a vulnerable creature in a universe that often seems capricious. Individual man is prone to accidents. His relationships with his kind are frayed by hostility and envy; often his own goals elude him while his fellows seem to achieve what they seek. Though there are observable regularities in nature, there are also sudden changes that are not unlike the outbursts of temperament that threaten the fragile order of society.

Yet man is a creature who has depended upon a degree of order for sheer survival. He has achieved it only imperfectly, but the need for it is embedded deeply within him. It is not the exclusive possession of self-conscious political regimes, and it extends beyond him to the cosmos. Folk explanations and the laws of science, myths and magic, the pantheons of gods and spirits, all are testimonies to a consuming search that expresses his inherent weakness as much as his evolutionary superiority.

The men of New Guinea know the tension of this common problem. Their answers to it are almost as different as the personal taste exhibited in body decoration, but whether the cosmos responds to the will of gods or ghosts or watchful nature spirits guarding their local fiefs like feudal lords, the world is perceived as a place that is under the governance of powers that transcend man's limitations. Earth is steeped in air.

In the highland valley of the Asaro River, the world is informed by an impersonal power whose presence is perceived in almost everything that men accomplish. The fertility of human beings, domestic animals, and crops; success in war; the accumulation of wealth—all the major goals that give direction to the culture—are dependent, in the long run, on the operation of this force of life, this ultimate, governing principle that is both remote from man yet also fused with his endeavors. It is the same throughout New Guinea. Not in the details of belief, which change from one group to another, but rather in the general statement of dependence—that man alone is inadequate, an earthbound creature in a universe that moves to a transcendental rhythm.

In each community, the grand occasions of life testify to this dependence. Whether they are celebrations of individual and group achievement, or rituals, such as male initiation, having to do with the passage of life, they are also affirmations, demonstrations, of the overriding sway of suprahuman power. For achievement itself is a vindication of the existence of such forces; it is not possible without their help.

While the beliefs and the symbols are exotic, the posture they represent is not so remote from our own experience as to be beyond our comprehension. Victors in wars of global magnitude solemnly attend *Te Deums* to give thanks for their deliverance, and it was not so long ago that respected Protestant divines gave God's sanction to the discrepancies of wealth developing in an expansionist and industrializing America.

New Guineans see the world in a similar way. Allowing for the over-simplification of complex views, each little system is invested with beliefs concerning the relationship between both personal and collective goals and this "other" governing order. The "big man" rises to his position of influence and eminence because of ambition, traits of personality, and his demonstrated acumen in husbanding and accumulating his personal resources, his managerial skills. Yet his very success relative to other men carries implications of special favor from the transcendental source of power, and so it is with the resonant festivals that climax the day-to-day routines of life. Scientists who have tried to immerse themselves in these cultures can see beyond the startling beauty of the resplendent human beings. Beneath the drumming and the stamping of feet, under the shrill singing, beyond the hypnotic tossing of plumes, they see the exemplification of a much broader and deeper-running pattern, the expression of a social order with a multitude of ties and goals that are intricately meshed with one another: family and extended groups of kinsmen, local oppositions and notions of man's nature. And all of this is imbued with air, encapsuled in imaginings that every human group has devised as answers to the perennial questions of who we are, what is our place in the universe, and what is the end of our brief journey.

New Guinea societies include no established priesthood, no religious roles that are totally supported by the faithful, no institutions similar to those of Buddhist Southeast Asia (or medieval-Christian Europe) where the religious life is a specialized vocation largely dependent upon the economic support of laymen. If one looks for familiar similes, the situation is closer to the original notion of Presbyterianism or the communal sects of our own time than to the entrenched hierarchy of the world churches with their specializations and ordered levels of authority. Dogma, the ultimate support of authoritarian religion, is not calcified in unquestionable codes, and the idea of heresy is therefore quite foreign to the people of New Guinea. They have never waged war to assert the supremacy of a particular religious "truth," have never felt compelled to impose their ultimate beliefs on others. They have perpetrated nothing remotely comparable to the "religious wars" that have torn Europe asunder and that resulted in the self-justifying extermination of ancient civilizations in the New World. Yet their view of life is religious. Man does not exist alone. He is not the measure of all things.

Rather, his achievements are possible only with the assistance of powers that transcend his limited capabilities. In a way that most of us have forgotten New Guineans experience this duality from day to day. Nature and supranature are not discrete realms. Everything is one, for earth is nothing without air.

Generally in New Guinea the ritual expression of this ultimate dependence is the responsibility of the males. New Guinean societies are male-dominated. Women have restricted roles in public affairs, though they exercise a considerable influence that often seems confounding to men, causing exasperation and not infrequent protest. But men rule in the area of religion. Characteristically, they alone are privy to the inner mysteries of the cults that celebrate the spiritual dimension of existence. Initiation, occurring in the early teens, admits them to a closed and privileged group that jealously guards its esoteric symbols, sometimes with threats of death to any female who may presume to look upon them. This discrimination is not unusual. There have been few religions that have not relegated women to merely minor roles. Roman Catholic nuns cannot offer Mass; Islam segregates women in the mosque; and no woman has risen above the rank of deacon in the Episcopal Church.

The reasons for this are lost in our beginnings. But, by and large, religion has been a man's world ever since our forebears emerged as a distinct species. Women have generally been subjected to the invidious status of a minority.

Male domination of the mythic, interstitial world of the spirit is most conspicuously revealed in cultures such as those along the Sepik River where magnificent cult houses, gabled like the cleaving and assertive prows of ships, are the local equivalent of the great church that dominates the clustered tenements of a Mexican village. Indeed, it is not stretching likeness too far to find a link between these buildings and Hagia Sophia in Istanbul, the first cathedral of Christendom. Mere size is irrelevant. The average Sepik cult house could rest quite comfortably between two of the vitreous columns supporting the first level of galleries under that cathedral's vast dome. Yet the cult houses dwarf their surroundings, their height and length expressing aspirations that have been enshrined in all the temples of the world.

If you enter these edifices, the similarity is inescapable. There is no stone and mortar. The vaults are exposed poles; the roofs and walls are thatch. But the buildings are filled with a cloistered light, a strange, noonday semidarkness that veils the painted bark-cloth hangings and the rows of images whose feet rest in a profusion of yellow gourds and strangely variegated aromatic leaves. Time and distance, geography and the accidents of history, fade before the palpable experience of something that is as old and as widely distributed as the human race. The cult house echoes with the hollow question that has been man's insistent companion through all the millennia

Men's cult-house on the Middle Sepik River; the largest of these structures now surviving, it is protected by the Australian government as a national monument

Detail of the foundation of a cult-house, intricately carved with human and anthropomorphic figures

46

Cult-house in the Chimbu highlands near Mount Wilhelm

of his existence. It is the same reverberating question posed by the prayer wheel at an isolated Himalayan pass, by the wayside cross and the tinseled household shrine, no less than by the florid magnificence of a Renaissance cathedral or the abstract spaces of a mosque.

One does not need to be familiar with the details of local belief in order to feel the breath of the cosmic wind. Stand before one of the great faces limned in the colors of the earth, russet, black, and ocher. To some of those

who view it, the stylized lines and one-dimensional planes suggest the conventions of gilded Byzantine mosaics and the icons of Eastern Orthodoxy. But under these cultural associations there lies a deeper level of recognition; one knows intuitively that this is the visage of everyman. The mouth is open under the elongated nose. Is it breathing, crying, or shouting to assert its will? The eyes are both reflective and resigned, troubled and compassionate—immemorial statements from the universal prison of a species.

Painted bark-cloth hangings and carved images in the men's cult-house at Maprik

This, perhaps, is the final word that the cultures of New Guinea—the cultures of the world—present to us. Differences in organization and material goals, in levels of technology and political aspirations, in convictions of what is right or wrong, in dogmas blindly adhered to as eternal truths, all, in a way, are accidents that have separated us from one another on a common

"Fresco" of bark-cloth paintings in an East Sepik cult-house

journey. The detours have carried us so far apart that it is often difficult to believe we started out together. Yet in the cult house, as in every shrine or sacred cave, one feels a kinship that continues to exist in spite of the Judas record of historical denials. The open mouth and enduring eyes of the primitive icon speak their message to the blood, to the complex chemistry we share with every member of our kind. It is there that recognition lies.

Earth and air have always formed the axis of the human world, and New Guinea is no exception. In the last analysis, it is no more than a localized expression of the brave and vaulting, tender and frustrating, questioning and hopeful course of a unique, self-aware creature endowed with prodigal gifts but condemned to a mortal prison.

Bark-cloth painting in the cult-house at Angoram

Bark mask, about 6 feet high, in a men's cult-house on the Sepik River

Facts and Figures

Geography. New Guinea is the largest of the many islands comprising the culture area of Melanesia. Melanesia (literally, "black islands") lies to the west of Polynesia and to the south of Micronesia. Together, the three culture areas make up the region generally referred to as Oceania.

Geographers identify three types of island in this vast area of the Pacific Ocean: high islands of volcanic origin (such as New Guinea and the Hawaiian group); coral atolls, formed from the calcified remains of marine organisms (the coral polyp); and makatea, uplifted coral atolls. The smallest are the coral atolls, which may be no more than one-half square mile in area and only a dozen feet, at their highest elevation, above sea level. At the opposite extreme, New Guinea measures about 306,600 square miles, with mountains rising to over 16,000 feet. Indeed, mountains are its most ever-present physical feature. Except for the estuaries and lower reaches of its great rivers (the Fly, the Sepik, the Ramu, the Markham, the Purari), it is a mass of tangled ranges clothed with dense jungle and interspersed with valleys, a spiny sea urchin sheltering approximately 1,167,000 human beings.

The isolating character of its formidable terrain has produced a fragmentation of languages and cultures unparalleled in any comparable area of the world.

Languages. There is no precise count of the number of localized languages spoken in New Guinea, but they may number between 700 and 1,000. Linguists separate them into two principal groups, Melanesian and Papuan, each of great diversity.

The Melanesian languages belong to the Malayo-Polynesian (Austronesian) family, which includes Indonesian, Polynesian, and Micronesian. They tend to predominate in coastal areas, in some of the island groups contiguous with the mainland, and in some low-lying valleys such as that of the Markham River. All are formally related to one another, though this does not mean that they are mutually intelligible. Relatively small local groups speak a vernacular different in many respects from that of their neighbors. The farther one moves from each localized "language center," the greater the vernacular differences and the impediments to verbal communication. The largest Melanesian-speaking group possessing a common language is probably the Tolai of New Britain, numbering about 35,000.

People speaking Papuan languages are far more numerous than the Melanesian-speakers, and there are many more such languages. Their highest concentration is in the highland regions stretching across the center of the country, though Papuan languages are also found interspersed with Melanesian both in other mainland areas and on contiguous islands. Papuan languages are sometimes designated as "non-Melanesian" or "non-Austronesian." Relationships between the Papuan languages are not yet clear, though a number of "families" are now being identified and further research may at last confirm the supposition, long held in abeyance, that all are related. Mutual unintelligibility, however, parallels the pattern for Melanesian languages, except that some linguistic groups are vastly greater in size than the largest group speaking a common Melanesian vernacular; for example, the Enga of the Western Highlands may number as many as 110,000.

The linguistic fragmentation has been a great barrier to communication among native New Guineans and between non-natives and the local population. Representatives of Western governments, missionaries, and those having commercial interests in the area were faced with virtually insurmountable difficulties. None of the indigenous languages was written, and to learn any individual dialect thoroughly would require time and skill and it would have had only localized utility. The need of non-natives to communicate with natives has spawned a number of lingua francas, such as Police Motu (in the southeast), Malay (in the west), and Melanesian Pidgin English (in the northeast).

Numerically, the most important is Pidgin English. Its vocabulary is drawn from many sources, but it is not merely a "jargon." It has considerable versatility and a formal structure similar to Melanesian languages. It must be learned; it cannot be approximated by merely adding "ums" and "ims" to familiar English words. For example, the opening lines of the funeral oration by Mark Anthony in Shakespeare's *Julius Caesar* would read like this in Pidgin:

> *Pren, man bolong Rom, Wantok, harim nau;*
> *Mi Kam tasol long plantim Kaesar. Mi noken beiten longen.*
> *Sopos sampela wok bolong wanpela man i stret; sampela i no stret;*
> *na man i dai;*
> *ol i waillis long wok i no stret tasol.*
> *Gutpela wok bolongen i slip;*
> *i lus nating long giraun wantaim long Kalopa.•*

•John J. Murphy, *The Book of Pidgin English* (Brisbane, Australia: W. R. Smith & Patterson, 1956).

Friends, Romans, countrymen, lend me your ears;
I come to bury Caesar, not to praise him.
The evil that men do lives after them;
The good is oft interred with their bones. . . .

Julius Caesar, Act III, Scene 2

Yet Pidgin has limited utility for a people who have begun to take their place in the modern world. It has no significant literature, particularly no scientific-technical literature. For most educated New Guineans, the language of the immediate future is likely to be English.

Physical types. The people of New Guinea are also physically diversified. They are probably an amalgam of a few racial stocks whose representatives found their way to the island long before the period of recorded history. These stocks no longer exist in any "pure" form, and scientific investigations have barely scratched the surface of genetic relationships. However, superficial differences tend to give the impression of many localized "physical types." Some of these observable differences are surely more apparent than real. Varied conventions of dressing and wearing the hair, of facial ornamentation and decoration, give the appearance of a greater diversity than actually exists, though there are certain identifiable extremes in physical characteristics.

Man from the Western Highlands, decorated for a festival

Cultures. Fragmentation is equally evident in the realm of customs, beliefs, and institutions. New Guinea contains a multitude of different localized cultures. Significant variations in the details of life occur over quite small distances. What one may learn about the culture of a particular group is unlikely to apply point by point to the people living beyond the next ridge. Indeed, the differences are so numerous that it may seem hazardous, perhaps impossible, to speak of "New Guinea culture" in any encompassing sense. Yet anthropologists know that the rich diversity is overlaid on a basic pattern that tends to "unify" the region and differentiates it as a whole from both Polynesia and Micronesia.

History. The discovery of New Guinea by Westerners is attributed to the Portuguese in 1511. Through the following centuries, it was visited by navigators such as the Spaniards Ynigo Ortiz de Retez (1546) and Luis Vaez de Torres (1606), the Dutchman Abel Janszoon Tasman (1643), the Englishman William Dampier (1700), the Frenchman Louis Antoine de Bougainville (1768), the Englishman James Cook (1770), and the French Chevalier Antoine d'Entrecasteaux (1793). However, it was not until the last half of the nineteenth century that it assumed much significance in the final chess game of old-style imperialism. By 1914 the mainland had been apportioned between three metropolitan powers: the Dutch, the Germans, and the Australians. The western half of the island was known as Netherlands (Dutch) New Guinea. The eastern half was divided between German New Guinea in the north and the Australian Territory of Papua in the south. This southeastern portion of the island had been annexed by Britain in 1888 and was known as British New Guinea from that time until metropolitan sovereignty was transferred to Australia in 1906.

Following the First World War, administrative responsibility for German New Guinea was transferred to Australia under a Mandate from the League of Nations. It became known as the Mandated Territory of New Guinea.

After the Second World War, Netherlands New Guinea remained for a time under Dutch control, though it was claimed by the newly independent Republic of Indonesia. The former Mandated Territory became a Trust Territory granted to the Commonwealth of Australia by the United Nations. Australia incorporated it into an administrative union with the Territory of Papua. Thenceforth, the eastern half of the main island, together with numerous off-shore island groups, was designated the Territory of Papua and New Guinea. Ultimately, the Dutch relinquished sovereignty over the western section, which became an integral part of the Republic of Indonesia and is known as West Irian (*Irian Barat*).

Suggestions for Further Reading

Fisk, E. K. (ed.). *New Guinea on the Threshold: Aspects of Social, Political and Economic Development.* Canberra, Australia: Australian National University Press, 1966.
>   A good collection of articles written by specialists for non-specialists.

Gardner, Robert, and Heider, Karl G. *Gardens of War: Life and Death in the New Guinea Stone Age.* New York: Random House, 1969.
>   Fine photographs taken among a group of Dani-speaking people in the Western Highlands, accompanied by informative essays. See also Matthiesen, *Under the Mountain Wall.*

Lea, D. A. M., and Irwin, P. G. *New Guinea: The Territory and Its People.* Melbourne, Australia: Oxford University Press, 1967.
>   Elementary coverage of geography and major subsistence patterns.

Malinowski, Bronislaw. *Argonauts of the Western Pacific.* New York: Dutton, 1961 (paperback).
>   Detailed study of Trobriand Island culture about the time of the First World War: a classic work in anthropology. The non-specialist may find some sections difficult.

Matthiesen, Peter. *Under the Mountain Wall: A Chronicle of Two Seasons in the Stone Age.* New York: Ballantine Books, 1969 (paperback).
>   Deals with the same Dani-speaking people as Gardner and Heider, *Gardens of War.* Not a scientific study but an episodic narrative conveying the personal world of some individuals.

Mead, Margaret. *New Lives For Old: Cultural Transformation—Manus 1928-1953.* New York: Dell, 1966 (paperback).
>   A rich description of radical culture change on Manus, one of the Admiralty Islands.

Newman, Philip. *Knowing the Gururumba.* New York: Holt, Rinehart and Winston, 1965 (paperback).
>   A short and readable study of a society in the Eastern Highlands.

Oliver, Douglas L. *The Pacific Islands.* Garden City, N. Y.: Natural History Press, 1961 (Anchor Books, paperback).
>   Introductory survey of Oceania as a whole, which helps place New Guinea in the context of the larger region.

Read, Kenneth E. *The High Valley.* New York: Charles Scribner's Sons, 1965 (Scribner Library paperback).

An account of the Gahuku people of the Eastern Highlands, presenting their culture through characterizations of individuals and detailed description of events in their lives.

Rowley, Charles. *The New Guinea Villager: The Impact of Colonial Rule on Primitive Society and Economy.* New York: Frederick A. Praeger, 1966.

A study of social and political changes in the Territory of Papua and New Guinea, presenting the history and current status of an emerging nation.

Souter, Gavin. *New Guinea: The Last Unknown.* New York: Taplinger, 1963.

Colorful and fascinating account of European contact and exploration in New Guinea.

Worsley, Peter. *The Trumpet Shall Sound: A Study of "Cargo" Cults in Melanesia.* New York: Schocken Books, 1968 (paperback).

Well-written general coverage of millenarian cults in New Guinea, by a specialist but addressed to the general reader.

INDEX

(Page numbers in italics refer to illustrations)

About the Photographer

George Holton is a freelance photographer whose specialties are primitive people, natural history, travel, and archaeology. His pictures have appeared in such national magazines as *Holiday, National Geographic* and *Time,* and his photographs of Easter Island are included in *Island at the Center of the World* by Father Sebastian Englert. He has also contributed articles to *Natural History* and *Life* magazines. A world traveler, Mr. Holton was born in the United States but now lives in Guatemala.

About the Author

Kenneth E. Read was born in Sydney, Australia, and came to the United States in 1957. He is at present Professor of Anthropology at the University of Washington, Seattle.

Before this, he was Senior Lecturer in Anthropology at the Australian School of Pacific Administration, Sydney, and Research Fellow of the School of Pacific Studies, the Australian National University, Canberra.

He was educated at the University of Sydney, where he received his M.A. in 1946, and at the University of London, England, where he received his Ph.D. in 1948.

An active contributor to anthropological literature, Professor Read is the author of *The High Valley* and has published a number of articles in technical and scholarly journals.